Copyright © 2021 by Penny Teague

All rights reserved. No part of this publication may be reproduced, distributed, or transmitted in any form or by any means, including photocopying, recording, or other electronic or mechanical methods, without the prior written permission of the publisher, except in the case brief quotations embodied in critical reviews and other noncommercial uses permitted by copyright law.

ISBN: 978-1-954341-99-9 (Paperback)
       978-1-63945-000-8 (Ebook)

The views expressed in this book are solely those of the author and do not necessarily reflect the views of the publisher, and the publisher hereby disclaims any responsibility for them.

Writers' Branding
1800-608-6550
www.writersbranding.com
orders@writersbranding.com

To my Daughters- Erin & Amber

I'm proud of you for being so strong and accomplishing so much even when the pain of a migraine tries to keep you down.

Mommy, I am sick.

Here baby, take this bowl in case you get sick again.

Okay, Mommy...

Baby, we need to take you to the doctor, nothing is breaking this migraine.

Okay Mommy, will it hurt?

Only a little baby, they're going to help.

Ma'am, how long has she had this migraine?

Three days.

Let's give her a shot of medicine and some steroids.

Okay Doctor, thank you for your help.

Mommy, will the shots hurt?

Just a little pinch and a sting, baby.

Goodnight. Get some rest, baby.
I will see you in the morning.

Okay Mommy, goodnight.

www.ingramcontent.com/pod-product-compliance
Ingram Content Group UK Ltd
Pitfield, Milton Keynes, MK11 3LW, UK
UKRC030205240426
12048UKWH00004B/88